What's inside?

Mindfulness What is it?

Mindfulness ... namby-pamby?
Monkey brain
Mindful or mind full? How does it help?

Emotions
- Emotions...what's the point!
- Basic emotions...What do they mean?
- 8 Basic emotions
- Complex emotions
- Positive and negative emotions
- Fight or Flight... freeze or Faint
- Emotional speedometer
- Take notice!

Mindfulness practices – Things that may help
- Identifying triggers
- 5 senses grounding technique
- STOP!!! Take a moment!
- Circle of Control

Breathing Techniques
- High 5 Breathing
- Belly breathing
- 5 Finger breathing

- Box breathing
- Pucker up breathing
- Body scan

Mindfulness practices – Stuff to do
- Keeping a diary
- Mantra pathways
- Colouring
- Cooking
- Social media – out with the old in with the new!
- Reflection
- Mindfulness walking
- Dog walking
- Go barefoot...Just watch the mindfulness dogs!
- Mindful music

Bed yoga
- Bed stretches
- Knee ups
- Side-lying quad stretch
- Child pose
- Cobra

30-day mindfulness challenge
Create your own 30-day mindfulness challenge

About the Author

Kim grew up on a council estate in Watford and spent her teenage years under the care of social services frequently relocating and wrestling with an unsettled existence. Her emotional struggles led her to drop out of school at 15 and later abandon her pursuit of art school.

At the age of 18, she relocated to Cardiff, many years later, through diligent self-work and determination, Kim obtained a BA (Hons) in youth and community. Gaining experience from assisting individuals dealing with substance misuse to supporting young people with additional needs. Her experience extends to working with students attending a pupil referral unit, aiding those at risk of or experiencing sexual exploitation, and supporting young individuals facing homelessness.

Her passion for supporting young people grew stronger, prompting her to pursue an MA in advanced youth and community and an MSc in Psychology (conversion). Kim currently works within police custody supporting 10 to 17-year-olds who find themselves entangled in the criminal justice system.

mindfulness
What is it?

Mindfulness ... namby-pamby?

Mindfulness doesn't have to be wishy-washy mumbo jumbo! Mindfulness means paying attention to what's happening both inside and outside of us, right now, in this moment. Sometimes we get so caught up in our thoughts that we forget to notice what's going on around us. This can make us feel disconnected from our bodies and our feelings.

Mindfulness helps us to tune back into our bodies and become more aware of what we're experiencing. We can do this by noticing how things feel, the sights, sounds, smells, and tastes of what's happening around us. For example, when you walk up the stairs, you might pay attention to the feel of the banister in your hand.

It's that simple!

Another important part of mindfulness is being aware of our thoughts and feelings as they happen. This means noticing when we're feeling happy, sad, angry, or anything else. By paying attention to our thoughts and feelings, we can learn to understand them better and make choices about how we react to them.

It's like being the captain of your own ship, instead of just going along for the ride.

Monkey Brain

The term "monkey brain" is often used to describe a feeling when our thoughts are jumping around like a bunch of monkeys swinging from tree to tree. Just like monkeys, our thoughts can sometimes be really fast and all over the place too! When we have a lot on our minds or we're feeling worried, our thoughts might feel like this, and we might find it hard to focus on one thing. But just like how monkeys can settle down and rest, we can also find ways to calm our minds.

Mindful or mind full?
How does it help?

Mindfulness can help you in several ways. Here are some reasons how it can help you:

- Reduces stress and anxiety: Mindfulness practices have been proven to lower stress and anxiety levels. By becoming more aware of your thoughts and emotions, you can learn to manage them in a healthy way.

- Improves focus and concentration: Mindfulness can help you improve your concentration and stay focused. By learning to bring your attention to the present moment, you can become better at avoiding distractions and staying on task.

- Better emotional regulation: When we feel loads of different emotions, it can be hard to control them. Mindfulness can help us to become more aware of these feelings and learn how to handle them in a healthy way. This means we can learn to feel calm and happy more often!

- Improve relationships: Do you ever feel like you're not really paying attention when you're talking to your family or friends? Mindfulness can help you to be more present and really focus on what they're saying. By doing this, you can improve your relationships with the people you care about. You'll be better at listening and understanding how they're feeling, which can help you communicate more effectively and be more empathetic. This can lead to stronger, more meaningful connections with others!

- Increased self-awareness and self-esteem: Mindfulness can help you become more aware of your strengths and weaknesses, as well as your values and goals. This can lead to increased self-esteem and a stronger sense of self.

Our sense of self is influenced through our relationships with others, for example, feeling happy when someone says something nice about us. It can also happen when we think about things that happened before, like feeling sad about hurting a friend's feelings in the past. These experiences help us understand how important it is to have good relationships with others, especially when we're young. They can teach us how valuable we are and help shape our sense of self.

Self-esteem is how we feel about ourselves, and it's important because it can affect how we see the world and how we interact with others. Having a strong sense of self means having a clear understanding of who you are, what you stand for, and what makes you unique.

When we have good self-esteem, we feel confident in our abilities and comfortable with who we are as a person. We don't try to compare ourselves to others or worry too much about what other people think of us. Instead, we focus on our own goals and passions, and we treat ourselves with kindness and respect.

Mindfulness can help us to develop better self-esteem and a stronger sense of self by teaching us to be more aware of our thoughts and feelings.

When we practice mindfulness, we learn to observe our thoughts without judging ourselves or getting too caught up in them. This can help us to let go of negative self-talk and become more accepting of who we are. With regular practice, we can build a stronger sense of self and feel more confident in our own skin.

Emotions

Emotions...What's the point!

It's important to learn how to control your emotions because they're linked to how you think and feel. This can help you make better decisions on how to respond to different situations. Basically, your thoughts and feelings have a big impact on your actions and how you behave. By learning how to regulate your emotions, you can make sure you're making good choices and acting in a positive way.

If we learn how to control our emotions, we can avoid making impulsive decisions that we might end up regretting later. Instead, we can make wise choices that can make our lives easier and improve our mental health. So, by regulating our emotions, we can make sure we're thinking things through and making choices that are good for us in the long run.

Basic Emotions...
What do they mean?

Your brain has 8 basic emotions that are built-in from the time you're born, which make your body react in different ways. These are:

- Anger: Feeling upset or angry in response to being hurt or wronged by someone.
- Joy: Feeling happy and content with ourselves and what we have.
- Fear: Feeling scared or worried about something we think might harm us.
- Sadness: Feeling unhappy or down, needing comfort and support from others.
- Anticipation: Excitedly looking forward to something we expect to happen.
- Surprise: The way we react when something unexpected or surprising happens.

- Disgust: a strong feeling of revulsion towards something that is offensive, unpleasant, or repulsive.
- Trust: Believing that something or someone is safe and won't cause harm.

8 Basic Emotions

Complex Emotions

Sometimes, emotions can combine to create new feelings. For example, when we feel nervous and excited at the same time, we might feel a combination of anticipation and fear. These are called complex emotions. These feelings are not already inside us when we are born, but we learn them from our families and surroundings as we grow up.

Basic & Complex Emotions

Basic Emotion

Joy

Its a pure emotion that stands alone

It can't be unpacked as its just 1 emotion

Complex Emotion

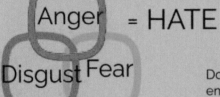

Anger

Disgust Fear

= HATE

Doesn't just happen, this emotion takes thinking about

Made up of more than 1 emotion

Positive and Negative Emotions

Positive emotions make us want to do things that made us happy before because they activate a part of our brain that makes us feel good and safe.

Negative emotions help us to be careful and avoid things that might be dangerous. Emotions have helped people stay safe and survive for a long time. Even though we don't face the same risks as our ancestors, emotions still help us understand our world and protect ourselves.

Fight or Flight... Freeze or Faint

When we sense danger, our body has a response called the "fight-or-flight" response. This helped our ancestors stay safe from danger a long time ago.

Nowadays, people can still have this same response triggered by situations where they feel threatened. This can make them feel more scared than they need to be, even if there isn't really a danger.

The fight-or-flight response is like an overprotective car alarm that goes off even if there's no danger to the car.

It's like our own personal alarm system, but sometimes it can make mistakes.
The good news is, just like you can fix a car alarm, you can also train your brain to figure out if a threat is real or not.

Emotional Speedometer

REDUCED SPEED AHEAD

What happened?　　　　　　　　　　　　Speed?

argued with mum	4

How did I react?　　　　　　　　　　　　Speed?

Smashed my room up	9

24

Take Notice!

1. One important skill to have is being able to recognize and identify your emotions. You can start by paying attention to how your body feels. Are you feeling queasy in your stomach? Is your heart beating faster than usual? Do you feel any tightness or pressure in your neck or head? By tuning in to your body, you can become more aware of your emotions and learn how to manage them better.

2. Once you've noticed what you're feeling, it's helpful to name it so that you can take control of the situation. Start by asking yourself what emotion best describes what you're feeling. Is it anger, sadness, disappointment, or resentment? Maybe it's a combination of different emotions. Remember that fear is a common emotion that often hides beneath others. Don't be

afraid to identify emotions you might be feeling. Once you've named them, try to dig deeper and understand why you're feeling that way. If you're feeling fear, what are you afraid of? If you're feeling anger, what is the cause of your anger? By understanding your emotions and their underlying causes, you can take a step closer to sharing your feelings with others.

3. Emotions are a natural and normal part of how we react to different situations. So, instead of criticizing yourself for feeling angry or scared, understand that your emotional responses are valid and understandable. It's important to practice self-compassion and give yourself some leeway. Remember that feeling emotions is a natural human reaction, and you're not alone in experiencing them.

Mindfulness can help you be present in the moment by focusing on your internal experiences. Use your senses to observe what's happening around you without judging it. These skills can help you stay calm and prevent negative thought patterns from taking over when you're feeling emotional pain. By practicing mindfulness, you can stay grounded in the present moment and avoid getting swept away by overwhelming emotions.

mindfulness practices

Stuff you can do!

little bit of calmness

Identifying Triggers

It's okay to feel negative emotions, and you don't have to avoid them. However, it's also important not to keep exposing yourself to situations that trigger unpleasant emotions.
Take some time to reflect on things that are present when you start feeling negative emotions. This requires being honest with yourself.

Did something happen that made you feel bad? Emotions often come from our hidden insecurities, especially ones that we haven't dealt with. So, pay attention to your surroundings and consider what past experiences might be coming up?

Hangry??

It's important to take notice of how you're feeling, including whether you're hungry or tired. These factors can intensify your emotions and cause you to perceive them more strongly than you would otherwise.

If you can address the underlying issue, such as eating when you're hungry or getting some rest when you're tired, it can change how you respond emotionally to situations. By taking care of your basic needs, you can improve your ability to regulate your emotions.

5 senses grounding technique

When you're feeling upset or overwhelmed, take a deep breath and do these steps to help you feel better:

5: Look around and find FIVE things you can see, like a chair or a book.

4: Touch FOUR things around you, like the soft cushion on the couch or a fluffy pillow.

3: Listen for THREE things you can hear, like birds chirping or music playing.

2: Take a sniff and smell TWO things, like fresh flowers or your favourite candle.

1: Finally, think of ONE thing you can taste, like a piece of gum or a sip of water.

This exercise can help you focus on what's happening around you right now and bring your mind to a calmer place.

STOP!!! Take a moment!

Do you ever feel like you need a moment to calm down and disconnect from others and reconnect with yourself?
The STOP method is a great way to do this!

Here's how it works:

(S) Stand up and take a deep breath.
(T) Tune into your body. Pay attention to how it feels, and any sensations you notice.
(O) Observe. What is your body trying to tell you?
(P) Ask yourself what's possible. What new things might happen if you take this moment to connect with yourself? How could this help you have a better day?

So, next time you need a break, remember to STOP and try this!

Circle of Control

The circle of control is a tool that can help you understand the things that are in your control and the things that are not. It's important to know this because it can help you focus your energy and efforts on the things that you can actually change.

The circle of control has three parts. The first part is the inner circle, which includes things that you have complete control over, like your thoughts, attitudes, and behaviours. This means that you can choose how you think, feel, and act in any situation.

The second part is the middle circle, which includes things that you can influence but cannot control, like your relationships with others or your marks at school. You may not have complete control over these things, but you can still make a difference by putting in the effort, communicating effectively, and seeking help when needed.

The third part is the outer circle, which includes things that are outside of your control, like the weather, other people's actions, or global events. These things are not in your power to change, so it's important not to worry too much about them.

By understanding the circle of control, you can focus on the things that are in your power to change, which can help you feel more confident, motivated, and in control of your life.

Circle of Control

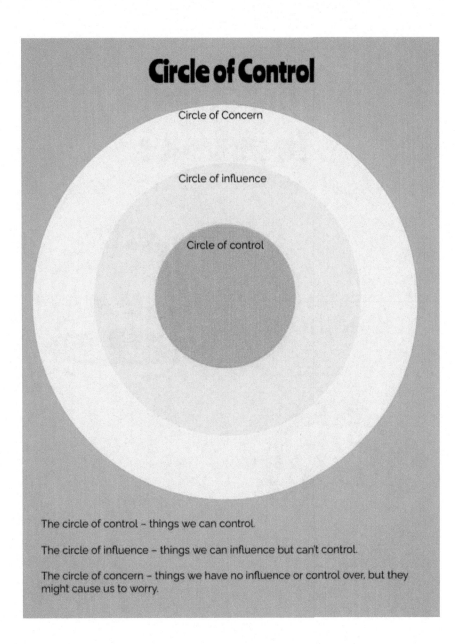

Circle of Concern

Circle of influence

Circle of control

The circle of control – things we can control.

The circle of influence – things we can influence but can't control.

The circle of concern – things we have no influence or control over, but they might cause us to worry.

Breathing Techniques

Breathe in....

And out...

High 5 Breathing

Inhale for a count of 5.
Exhale for a count of 5.

Do this for at least a few minutes.... Simple!!

Belly Breathing

Your body has a muscle that helps you breathe called the diaphragm, it's shaped like a dome. When you take a deep breath in, your diaphragm gets tighter and moves down, making more room for your lungs to fill up with air. Then, when you breathe out, your diaphragm relaxes and moves back up in your chest.

This way of breathing is called diaphragmatic breathing, also known as "belly breathing" or "abdominal breathing." When we breathe like this, it helps us get more oxygen into our body and get rid of old air (carbon dioxide). This kind of breathing can make our heart beat slower and even help our blood pressure stay at a good level. It's good for everyone to learn how to breathe like this!

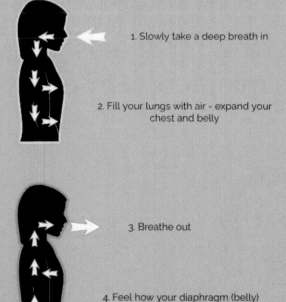

1. Slowly take a deep breath in

2. Fill your lungs with air - expand your chest and belly

3. Breathe out

4. Feel how your diaphragm (belly) contracts inwards

5 Finger Breathing

Five-finger breathing is a mindfulness technique designed to learn how to pause and take five deep breaths using your fingers. It's a convenient practice that can be done anytime, anywhere.

Box Breathing

Did you know that Navy SEALS use this breathing exercise to stay calm and focused in tough situations? It can help slow down your heart rate and blood pressure, which makes you feel more relaxed and able to think more clearly.

Breathe in for 4 seconds, hold your breath for 4 seconds, breathe out for 4 seconds, and hold your breath for 4 seconds again.

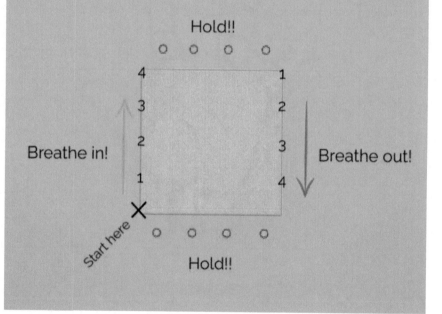

Pucker up Breathing

Start by loosening up your neck and shoulders, then breathe in gradually through your nostrils while keeping your mouth shut for two counts.
After that, make your lips pucker up as if you were going to whistle and blow out slowly by exhaling air through your pursed lips for four counts

Body Scan

1. Get comfortable. Lie down or sit in a position that allows you to stretch your limbs easily.
2. Close your eyes and begin focusing on your breath. Notice the sensation of your breath filling and leaving your lungs as you inhale and exhale.
3. Choose where to start. Begin anywhere you like — the top of your head, or the bottom of your feet.
4. Focus on that spot as you continue breathing slowly and deeply. Pay attention to any feelings of pain, tension, discomfort, or anything out of the ordinary.
5. Spend anywhere from 20 seconds to 1 minute observing these sensations.
6. Continue breathing, imagining the tension decreasing with each breath.
7. when your thoughts start to drift, gently return your thought to the scan.
8. Once you finish scanning parts of your body, just stay there while your comfortable
9. Slowly release your focus and bring your attention back to your surroundings.

Remember to take your time and enjoy the experience. You can practice this technique whenever you want to feel more relaxed and focused.

Keeping a Diary.

Keeping a diary might sound a bit old-fashioned, but trust us, it's a game-changer! Whether you're stressing about exams, dealing with personal issues, or just feeling a bit lost, putting your thoughts down on paper can help you cope and find clarity. And guess what? Science backs this up too!

Writing in a diary can help reduce stress, manage anxiety, and even fight depression. It's easy to get started too — just grab a diary or notepad from your local Poundland, or if you're more tech-savvy, use a digital document.

Don't worry about spelling, grammar, or editing. Just write whatever comes to your mind, without any filters. It's your personal space to express yourself, without anyone judging you. Then, when you revisit your journal, you'll be amazed at how much you've grown and learned...Or if you don't want to keep it after, screw it up!! Throw it away!!

If you don't want to write, try recording a voice diary on your phone!

So why not give it a go?

Mantra Pathways

Do you ever feel like you're stuck in a negative spiral? Well, it's time to take control! Mantras are a powerful way to bring positivity and confidence into your life.

Repeating things can help your brain learn and get better. When you repeat words, movements, or thoughts, it creates new pathways in your brain that make you better at things. This is how we learn and re-learn things that we might have forgotten.

Mantras can be as simple or complex as you like, and you can say them in different ways. The important thing is that you say them out loud, so you can feel the vibrations of the words. This can help you become more self-aware.

Pay attention to what you're saying, focus on each syllable. Don't just say them without thinking! Really listen to how the words sound ... Is it starting to sound weird?

Give it a try. Choose a phrase or a favourite song that means something to you and repeat or sing it every day. You'll be amazed at how much it can change your outlook and help you achieve your goals.

Colouring

Colouring is one of the easiest ways to achieve mindfulness there are loads of adult colouring books available now, just find one you like, and try to look for books with intricate patterns, mandalas, or swirls.

The best part? It's well easy! Just grab some coloured pencils, markers, or pens, and start colouring the designs. As you focus on the colours and patterns, your mind should relax, and you'll feel a little calmer, it's a great way to destress

There are no rules when it comes to colouring – you can use whatever colours you like, and there's no right or wrong way to do it. It's a chance to tap into your creativity and express yourself.... If you want to colour a green cat...so be it!

So why not give colouring a go? It's a fun and creative way to de-stress and improve your mental health.

Cooking

Cooking can be mindful, but sometimes our minds can wander off and make us lose focus. Mindful cooking means paying attention to all the little details of what you're doing, like chopping, slicing, whipping, marinating, kneading, or tasting.

When you're mindful, you're really tuning into your senses - what you see, hear, smell, and feel - and focusing on the task at hand. This can make you feel calmer and more focused in the kitchen, and who knows, it might even make your food taste better!

It's easy to get distracted while cooking, but with mindfulness techniques, you can stay present and enjoy the process more.

Social Media – Out with the old, in with the new!

We know social media is a big part of your life, but have you ever thought about how it's affecting your well-being? Taking a closer look at a social media audit can be a game-changer.

We're not saying you should ditch social media altogether, but it's worth checking in with yourself to see if it's really serving you. Are you following accounts that inspire and uplift you? Or are you getting sucked into drama and negativity? It's time to take control of what you're seeing and how it's making you feel.

So, grab your phone and start auditing your social media accounts. Unfollow anyone who's bringing you down or causing you unnecessary stress. Instead, follow accounts that make you feel good and align with your interests and values.

Remember, social media can be a great tool for staying connected and finding inspiration. But it's up to you to make sure it's a positive force in your life. Start your social media audit today and take charge of your mental health!

Tips

Tip 1: Make a list of all the social media platforms you use, even include any that you have an account for but don't use regularly.

Tip 2: For each platform, ask yourself the following questions:
- Do I enjoy using this platform?
- Does it make me happy?
- Do I use it to compare myself to others?
- Do I spend more time on it than I'd like to?

Tip 3: Based on your answers, you should decide if you want to keep using it or take a break from it.

Tip 4: Set a few rules for yourself if you decide to keep using a site. You could, for example, limit yourself to checking it once a day or make it a rule not to scroll through your feed before bed.

Tip 5: Finally, unsubscribe from any accounts that regularly share negative or triggering information. On platforms like Facebook, you can block users or temporarily silence posts from certain people if their posts are causing you to worry. On Instagram, you can make your profile private, giving you more control over who can see your posts, who can send you messages, and add you. This is your space!

Reflection

Have you ever had a movie or song that hit you right in the feels? It's a great feeling, but sometimes you might not have someone to share it with. Don't worry though, taking some time to reflect on your experience can be just as rewarding.

Here are some questions you can ask yourself after watching or listening to something:

- What was it about?
- What parts stood out to you?
- Why did these parts stand out to you?
- How did it make you feel?
- Did it remind you of anything in your own life?

You can write down your thoughts in your diary or talk to a friend about it.

You could also share your thoughts on social media and start a discussion? Just don't get dragged into drama!

Mindfulness walking

Get some exercise while also practising mindfulness.

Mindful walking might be just what you need! It's easy to do, and you don't need any special equipment or skills to get started.

- **Step 1**: Find a quiet place to walk where you can fully focus on your surroundings. If you're outside, choose a path or trail that you know so you can relax and enjoy your walk.

- **Step 2**: Start walking and pay attention to your body. Notice how your feet feel as they touch the ground, how your legs are moving, and how your breath is flowing.

- **Step 3**: As you continue walking, take in the sights, sounds, and smells around you.

Be present in the moment and let yourself be fully aware of your surroundings. If your mind starts to wander, bring it back to the present moment.

Mindful walking can turn an everyday boring activity into a calming experience. So, grab some comfy shoes, find a nice spot, and start walking!

Dog Walking

Dogs are the Yoda's of mindfulness; they're constantly reminding us to live in the moment.

Dogs can be great mentors when it comes to mindfulness.

Dogs give us lots of chances to practice mindfulness every day. For example, when they want to play or go outside, we can stop what we're doing and be present in the moment with them.

Scientific research proves that spending time with dogs can make us feel happier and less stressed. Studies have shown that when we spend time with dogs, it can make a chemical in our bodies called oxytocin go up, which is a happy hormone. And it can make another chemical called cortisol go down, which is a stress hormone. So, spending time with dogs is good for us!

Go barefoot... Just watch the mindfulness dogs!

When you walk barefoot, focus on sensations you might not normally notice.

To get started, take off your socks and shoes and walk around on the carpet grass or floor. Notice how it feels. Can you feel any other surfaces to step on? Wiggle your toes and move your feet as you slowly walk around and pay attention to the experience of walking.

Going barefoot can help you in many ways!

It can help you have better control over where your feet land when you walk or run.

It helps your brain better understand where your body is in space, which can improve your movement and balance. It helps keep all the parts of your foot, ankle, knees, hips, and back healthy!

Scientific research has shown that going barefoot can help make your body stay stronger and healthier. It makes your immune system stronger by changing the amount of white and red blood cells in your body, making your body better at fighting off germs and helping you sleep better at night.

It can even help reduce swelling in your body and make you feel more relaxed.

Mindful Music!

Listening to music is really good for us! It can make us feel happy and less stressed. Music can even make different parts of our brain work better, like the parts that help us feel emotions, think, and move. Sometimes music can make us cry or want to dance because it's so powerful!

No matter what kind of music we like, we can enjoy it even more if we listen to it carefully and pay attention. This means really focusing on the music and being in the moment. By doing this, we can feel calmer and happier and appreciate how special music is to us.

Here are some tips for listening to music mindfully:

- Pick a song you like and find a quiet spot where you won't be interrupted. Take a deep breath and get comfortable.

- Pay attention to your body. Notice how it feels and take a few more deep breaths to relax.
- Now it's time to listen to the music! You can use headphones if you want, and even close your eyes if you want.
- As you listen, pay attention to what you notice. Maybe it's the guitar solo or the drumbeat. Does the music make you feel happy or sad? Just notice what comes up without judging yourself.
- After the song is over, take a moment to reflect on how you feel. Do you feel more relaxed or calm? Did you like the song you chose, or would you pick a different one next time?

Remember, listening to music mindfully can help you feel better and appreciate the music even more!

The music you choose to listen to is completely up to you.

Bed Yoga

if you find it hard to get up in the morning because you feels stiff and knackered, there's an easy way to fix this! All you need to do is stretch a bit before getting out of bed.

Stretching helps wake up your body and gets your blood flowing. It also activates the "rest and digest" system, which helps you feel more relaxed and calm right from the start of your day.

So, give it a try and see how much better you feel!

Bed Yoga
Stretches

Before you get out of bed try doing some simple stretches to get your body moving!

While lying down, bend your knees and lift your feet off the bed. Move your feet up and down, roll your ankles, and move them back and forth.

Look left and right slowly, roll your shoulders a few times, and work your arms by doing biceps curls with both hands. Don't forget to flex your wrists and open and close your hands a few times.

Bed Yoga to Try

Knee ups

Lie on your back with your legs straight out in front of you. Bend your left knee and hold the back of your thigh with your hands. Gently pull your knee towards your chest. Keep your right leg straight and point your toes towards the bottom of the bed. You should feel a stretch in the front of your right hip and thigh.

Relax and then switch sides to stretch your other leg.

Side-lying quad stretch

Lie on your right side with your legs straight and on top of each other. Rest your right arm under your head for support. Bend your left knee and bring your heel towards your left bottom. Reach behind with your left hand and hold onto your foot. You should feel a stretch in the front of your thigh and hip. Roll over onto your left side and repeat the stretch on your other leg.

Child's pose

Face down on your hands and knees with your knees hip-width apart and put your big toes together. Make sure your head and neck are in a good position. Move your bottom back slowly towards your heels while stretching your hands out in front of you. Rest your forehead on the bed. You should feel a stretch in your arms, shoulders, and back.

Cobra

Lie face down again with your legs straight and your toes pointing.

Place your hands just below your shoulders with your palms down on the bed. Press your palms into the bed to slowly lift your head, shoulders, and chest off the bed.

You should feel a stretch in the front of your torso and across your chest.

Take it easy and stop if you feel any discomfort.

30-day mindfulness challenge

A 30-day mindfulness challenge is a great way to start practicing daily activities that can help you reduce stress and anxiety.

By taking this challenge, you'll learn practical tools and strategies that you can use to feel more focused and present in your life.

It's a fun and rewarding way to take care of your mental and emotional health, and it can help you feel more peaceful and grounded in your daily life.

You can also create your own 30-day mindfulness challenge that is personalised to your own needs and interests.

30 Day Challenge

Mindfulness is also about finding things that you enjoy and being in that moment ....here are some ideas to get you started

Cook something new	Create a playlist	Find a game you enjoy on your phone	Do bed yoga	Go for a walk (with a dog)
Do a random act of kindness	Meet up with a friend	Declutter a corner of your room	Set a goal	Create something new
Practice breathing	Listen to a podcast	Try something new to eat	Take a relaxing bath or shower	Declutter a corner of your room
Go Barefoot	Reflect on a song or film	Go for a walk	Turn your phone off for 1 hour	Drink water
Declutter a corner of your room	Social media sort out	Eat slower	Turn the TV off	Do nothing!
Spend 1 day off social media	Do some gardening	Learn a new skill	Declutter a corner of your room	Do 5 senses grounding

Your 30 Day Challenge

start planning your own 30 day challenge

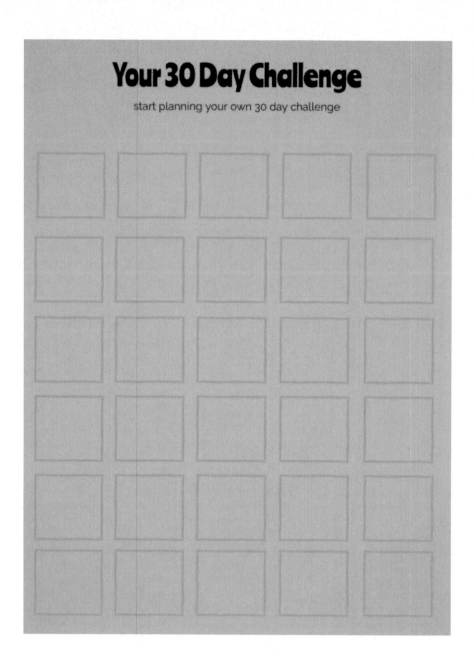

Mindfulness is a tool that can help you navigate the ups and downs of life. Throughout this book, we've explored just a few mindfulness techniques, but remember, mindfulness is not just a skill, it's a way of life.

As you finish this book keep these principles in mind:

Practice: Just like any skill, mindfulness improves with practice. Find time each day to cultivate mindfulness, even if it's just for a few minutes.

Embrace Imperfection: Don't strive for perfection in your mindfulness practice. It's okay to have wandering thoughts or challenging moments. The key is to notice them without judgment and gently bring your attention back to the present.

Be Kind to Yourself: Self-compassion is a must in mindfulness. Treat yourself with the same kindness and compassion that you would treat a friend.

Connect with Others: Mindfulness isn't just about self-improvement; it can also help you build deeper connections with friends and family.

Stay Curious: Mindfulness is a lifelong journey of self-discovery and exploration. Stay curious and open to new experiences.

Remember that mindfulness can be your anchor, it's a skill that will serve you not only now but throughout your entire life. So, I encourage you to continue exploring mindfulness, even if it's doing 1 or 2 of these exercises a day or a week.

Thank you for coming on this journey with me.

Keep Shining

Printed in Great Britain
by Amazon

30304723R10046